Boy Racer's
Handbook

Kevin S. Court

Virgin

Jonny B and Tim P – Cheers, lads.

This edition first published in Great Britain in 1996 by
Virgin Books
an imprint of Virgin Publishing Ltd
332 Ladbroke Grove
LONDON W10 5AH

First published in 1995 by Pulp Publishing (Over 5 copies sold!)

A catalogue record for this book is available from the British Library.

ISBN 0–7535–0023–X

Phototypeset by Intype London Ltd
Printed and bound by Mackays of Chatham PLC

**With special thanks to the Polar dealership, York, for letting
Kevin cane their Escort Cosworth for the cover of the first
Boy Racer's Handbook.**

To whoever cut me up at the lights.

ABOUT THE AUTHOR

Kevin Simon Court was born in Dagenham, Essex, on the 7th April 1971. His first car was a Mark I Ford Escort which had belonged to his brother when wearing a gold chain outside your Pringle jumper was considered the height of fashion. After stuffing that (whilst showing off to some birds) he purchased a Mark III Escort XR3i, which he still has. However, now that there is nothing else to modify on it, he is looking around for something else. In the unlikely event that 1) this book sells and 2) Kevin receives any dosh from his publisher, he will buy an Escort Cosworth. Or at least that rear wing to go on his Mark III.

ALSO BY THE AUTHOR

That ram raid at Dixons last month.

INTRODUCTION

Most driving manuals are serious works that lecture safety and expertise.

Not this one.

The Boy Racer's Handbook is an antidote to the woolly-pullied texts that learners swear by. Wrist-slapping accident statistics are nowhere to be found, nor are boiled-sweet-induced profundities concerning advanced driving technique.

Instead, the lighter side of motoring is explored in grim detail . . . Tartan Rugs, Fluffy Dice, Reliant Robins . . . from the red-mist tinged viewpoint of an avid Boy Racer.

Read it. Before the driver next to you at the lights does.

Bernd Dunlops, Institute of Advanced Boy Racers

'Animals'

ABS

Another Bloody Safety-feature. A killjoy
invention designed to prevent the wheels from
locking under heavy braking, rendering laddish
stops (see *The Professionals* or *The Sweeney*)
impossible.

ACCELERATOR

THE ACCELERATOR IS THE PEDAL ON THE RIGHT

(That was a public information message for the
benefit of old people)

As well as making the car go faster, our floor-
hinged friend performs several other useful
functions:

FRIGHTENING PEDESTRIANS

Pump the accelerator when pedestrians traverse
zebra crossings. Victims' reactions vary
accordingly, but all are amusing. Simultaneous
flashing of the headlights may expose
epileptics. Faster pedestrian clearance can be
achieved by moving the car forwards
menacingly. (If you happen to mow down the
slow, simply claim 'natural selection').

INDICATION OF LADDISHNESS

Similar technique to above, but practised at
traffic lights. Usually used in conjunction with

INCHING(qv). The driver in the lane alongside will thus be warned of your Boy Racing intentions (something to do with taking the side of your car off rather than letting him out-drag you).

ACCESSORIES

You are what you drive. Just look at Volvos and their drivers: Safe; Unassuming; *Boring*. Surely a case of like owner like car. Peugeot 205 GTis are youthful and exuberant. So's the maniac behind the wheel. And Porsches are seen by some to be phallic symbols, which figures.

But sometimes mass-produced cars cannot adequately convey the 'personality' of the owner. A little help is needed in the form of after-market accessories . . .

STICKERS are probably the cheapest and most accessible add-ons around. Sadly. They should satisfy a number of criteria:*

1. *The 'humorous' slogan*. Vulgar and/or chauvinistic examples only, please;
2. *Potent adhesive*. Strong enough to ensure paint and fingernail removal if any attempt is made to remove the sticker;
3. *Impairment of visibility*. Rearward vision *must* be kept to a minimum. Traces of sunlight indicate the need for another layer of laminate.

*The exception is, of course, the 'Darren-Sharon' sun strip, which (by way of special pardon) need not comply with condition no.1.

Stickers: Say goodbye to your fingernails.

Stickers to avoid at all costs:
- Anything *Green*. Especially the wanky 'Nuclear Power No Thanks' and even wankier 'Save the Rainforests'. See your nearest 2CV for further examples;
- Keep Your Distance stickers. (Unless of the laddish variety – 'If You're Reading This I'll Slam On The Anchors');
- All those starting 'I ♥';
- Those that have anything to do with horses. Or dogs.
- Initials. Save these for the leatherette briefcase.

Much more representative of boy racing tendencies are GO-FASTER STRIPES. However, when attempting to increase a vehicle's performance by borrowing features from a rally car, fitting the *engine*, not the sodding team colours, would be more effective.

Some Boy Racers have progressed from mere stripes and stickers, affixing more substantive emblems to their cars. DECALS are meant to enhance aesthetics, but like their human counterparts, tattoos, the owner often gets bored with the design and tries (completely unsuccessfully) to have it removed (see *Potent Adhesive*, overleaf). And remember – careful car/decal harmonisation is essential. Golden Eagle designs look more impressive on mud-encrusted Jeep Wranglers than on Fiat Pandas.

Other accessories include . . .

Garfield: Shats stuffing if you drive quick enough.

The GARFIELD. With wide eyes, clenched teeth and a tortured face pressed hard against triplex, the passenger of a Boy Racer bears a startling resemblance to this furry mascot. But the similarity ends there. Garfield never chunders. Not even when you're pulling 2g.

FLUFFY DICE. Deserving of their own separate entry. See FLUFFY DICE.

WAVING HANDS. Rarely seen nowadays, but not forgotten by anyone who's waved back at one. Achieved brief period of notoriety when an old lady at a zebra crossing stepped into the path of a ten-ton truck after misinterpreting the oscillating Hand as a courtesy gesture.

It's not all style-over-function, though. Oh no.

DOOR-EDGE PROTECTORS (*'fingers' type only*). Traditionally the domain of the sad and anally-retentive, door-edge protectors can now be purchased without embarrassment – thanks to the 'fingers' design. The laddish amputation joke assured a cult following, but luckily John Wayne Bobbit has yet to start merchandising in this area.

Unfortunately, the world of SEAT COVERS has regressed. Once available in classic orange 'tiger fur' trim, seat covers have now been superseded by ergonomic Yin-Yang ethno-beads. These are purchased by hippies who don't realise that abacuses are for counting on – not sitting on.

THE FLUFFY STEERING-WHEEL COVER, like the beaded seat cover, is unlikely to be found in a Boy Racer's car. This is because fluffy steering-wheel covers are for women who get cold hands and Welshmen who like the feel of wool. Not those who subscribe to the three Ps (Pint, Pull, Phal) on a night out.

ACCIDENTS

If you have an accident, say to yourself:

- It wasn't your fault;
- You couldn't have avoided it;
- Lots of good drivers have crashes – look at Nigel Mansell;
- You've had 'your accident' now, there won't be another;
- It was beneficial – you learn from your mistakes

. . . and try to forget that:

- You were completely and utterly to blame;
- You could have avoided it if you were
    - a) sober
    - b) driving more slowly
    - c) not adjusting your stereo
    - d) not trying to overtake me
    - e) Nigel Mansell;

- Things tend to come in threes;
- You didn't last time

. . . and that:

- You're due in court tomorrow;
- The insurance company has thought of a number, doubled it, added a few zeros, squared it – and then called the result your 'renewal premium'.

The Accident can take many forms, from the slow speed parking nudge to the head-on collision (see DAISIES, PUSHING UP . . .). But whatever accident you're planning to have, always consult *The Boy Racer's Handbook Accident Flowchart*:

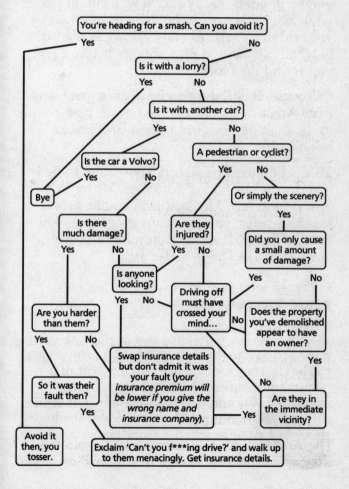

You're heading for a smash. Can you avoid it?
— Yes — No
Is it with a lorry?
Yes — No
Is it with another car?
Yes — No
A pedestrian or cyclist?
Yes — No
Or simply the scenery?
Yes
Is the car a Volvo?
Yes — No
Bye
Is there much damage?
Yes — No
Are they injured?
Yes — No
Did you only cause a small amount of damage?
Yes — No
Are you harder than them?
Yes — No
Is anyone looking?
Yes — No
Driving off must have crossed your mind... — No
Does the property you've demolished appear to have an owner?
Yes
So it was their fault then?
Yes
Swap insurance details but don't admit it was your fault (*your insurance premium will be lower if you give the wrong name and insurance company*). — No
Are they in the immediate vicinity?
Yes
Avoid it then, you tosser.
Exclaim 'Can't you f***ing drive?' and walk up to them menacingly. Get insurance details.

ADVANCED DRIVING

Advanced Driving is the complete opposite of
Boy Racing. Advanced Driving is all about
woolly jumpers, cords and 'a nice cup of tea
while we see what can be done to improve
your driving', whereas Boy Racing is shellsuits,
baseball caps and 'a pint of lager before I race
you round the block'.

Of course, Boy Racers could learn a great deal
from Advanced Drivers (like how to bore people
to death at parties), but tuition isn't just an
option.

This is because Boy Racers know how to drive
– and won't be taking advice on Mirror Signal
Speed from nice Mr Cardigan, thanks very
much. Besides, you can learn everything you
need to know about car control in a single
episode of *The Dukes of Hazzard*.

ADVERTISING

Apparently, the Volvo 850 drives like it's alive.
But what about the driver? He drives like he's
brain dead.

Daredevil stuntmen? Come on, lads. No Volvo
driver I know can get their car down the high
street in a straight line, let alone across a canyon.

That said, some ads do tell the truth. The Citroen

Xantia was promoted with the line 'Even standing still it's moving'.

It suffered from the occasional handbrake failure.

AIRBAG

An essential option for Family Man, but not the Boy Racer. Polo-sized Mountneys are preferred (they look better, especially when worn on the forehead).

AIR CONDITIONING

The stage after shampooing for all a Boy Racer would know. A grand's a lot of money to pay for a fridge when you've got windows to open. And what are those blue segments by your air vents for? Geography questions?

ALARMS

There are two types of car alarm – the cheap *'scare 'em off'* alarm – and the expensive *'nick the alarm and leave the car'* alarm. The first type may not even function, simply being a dummy system. But it doesn't really matter. The working ones are just as ineffective – a thief would have to open all the doors, sound the horn and ask politely to trip the switch. If you're lucky.

The second type of alarm doubles your car's value on installation. They have to be fitted by someone with a Tefal slap and a PhD in Electronics. Unfortunately, they also have to be set by one (which is just as well because they require a urine sample and sliver of DNA to disarm).

The cheaper security systems are often tremor sensitive, which means you'll be alerted to the presence of heavy lorries and falling leaves near your car. More useful is the ultrasonic device, which warns of stiff breezes. Microwave systems are less paranoid though, and defrost thieves into the bargain.

ALCANTARA

Suede-like synthetic fabric used to upholster cars. Expensive, but cheapened by a name that sounds like a resort on the Costa del Concrete. Allegedly fades in sunlight, but as I drive in England I wouldn't know.

AMBULANCE

Tearing past slow vehicles on the wrong side of the road . . . jumping traffic lights . . . breaking the speed limit . . . Boy Racing's not a crime – it's a qualification.

An ad placed in *Max Power* should be enough to staff the ambulance service for decades.

ANCHORS

Ladspeak for the brakes.

ANECDOTES

The Boy Racer invariably has a few 'memorable' anecdotes to impress his mates – always involving either nearly getting booked or nearly getting killed. Tradition insists that the Boy Racing anecdote is enormously exaggerated and only bears token resemblance to the truth. The account should begin with the phrase 'You're not going to believe this . . .' because stating the obvious can sometimes fool listeners for a moment or two.

ANIMALS

NAME	DESCRIPTION	HABITAT	ACTION
HORSE	Tall, with swishing tail. Dumps on the move. Piloted by Doris with fat thighs.	Country lanes. Look for tell-tale muck trail.	Sounding horn and revving engine makes them uneasy. Sound horn and rev engine.
DOG	Hairy quadruped that barks a lot. Scatty. Moults. Farts.	Occasionally in road, trying to get run over. Sometimes in car with head out of window, tongue flapping in the slipstream.	If in road, avoid (they can do serious damage to your car). If in car ignore – but watch that electric window button!
CAT	Small, moody, agile creature that makes insurance salesmen look trustworthy. Eyes glow in dark, making them easier to mow down at night. (Sadly, insurance salesmen are harder to identify for this purpose).	On or up anything climbable, so rarely found on road. Characteristic dirty paw-marks indicate their presence on top of vehicle.	Electrify car body to deter cats from sullying your car's paintwork.
RABBIT	Furry, with big ears. Lives underground.	Grassy areas and hedgerows at the side of the road.	No action needed. Stupid enough to get run over by themselves.
HAMSTER	Small rodent with big cheeks.	In cages and pet shops. Up celebrities' bottoms.	Soft fur ideal for polishing car bodywork or for mopping condensed windows.

NAME	DESCRIPTION	HABITAT	ACTION
PIGEON	Grey bird with nodding head. 'Coo-ing' call guaranteed to annoy.	Normally in the middle of the road, for some reason. Also found in pedestrian precincts and on pavements.	Despite their dozy state they normally fly away just before a car hits them. Unfortunately.
SHEEP	Woolly. Makes silly bleating noise.	Fields, moors, moor-roads, farmers' Wellington boots.	Only if you're a farmer.
COW	Leather-covered milk-machine. Moos.	Fields, country lanes (if being shepherded by yokel).	You must be joking. If you encounter a herd of these in a narrow lane don't make any plans (apart from washing your muck-encrusted car when you eventually get home).
HEDGEHOG	Flat.	Road surface.	Leave it there. Some granny will soon be along with a saucer of milk to try and revive it.
ROADHOG	Inconsiderate driver who takes up more road than he needs.	The middle lane of motorways.	The finger.
ROAD-RUNNER	Fast, brightly-coloured ostrich. Meep-Meep call.	The desert, near cliffs with easily dislodged ledges.	Try something out of the ACME catalogue.

ANTI-FREEZE

Liquid the same colour as a strawberry Slush Puppy, but probably better tasting. Never store in a bottle marked *Lemonade*. (Forget the kids . . . you should see what fizzy drink can do to an engine.)

ARMCO

Corrugated crash barrier. Notorious for being the only aspect of a Scalextric track that nobody could be arsed with.

B

'Bucket Seats'

BACK-UP

The most dangerous traffic jams are those which occur on the motorway. People expect the cars in front to be moving, not parked (unless it's the M25).

The fast lane is often the first to back-up. Which is unfortunate because this is the lane that Paul-the-Rep cruises at 115 in. However, he does do 200,000 motorway miles a year, so he shouldn't be a problem. The biggest liability is probably the GRANDAD (qv) who cruises at minimum fuel consumption and spends most of his braking distance with his head in the glove compartment searching for boiled sweets.

Of course, some drivers love back-ups. The family man, for example, lives for that smug feeling of community duty that he gets when he uses his hazard-lights to indicate heavy braking.

BATTERY

That box under the BONNET (qv) which has a black and a red lead attached to it. Powers the starter motor and the in-car electrics, so Japanese cars must have a bloody big one. Typically flat when you need it most.

BODYKIT

Automotive stone-cladding. Consists of:
1) A **Front Airdam**, which is deep enough to frighten off a squadron of Lancasters with bouncing bombs;
2) **Side Skirts** set lower than Victorian hemlines; and
3) the massive **Rear Wing**, to help reduce rear visibility even further.

It should be noted that Boy Racers will add bodykits to bodykits until the desired look is achieved.

BOLLARD

Dirty great lumps of concrete designed to prevent you from taking corners with two wheels on the pavement. Also awkward to reverse round when you have a crack at Currys with the Transit.
Also see CONES, TRAFFIC.

BONNET

Vent and scoop for a 'muscle-car' image (easily achieved using a drill, hacksaw, Cornflakes packet, and some double-sided sticky-tape). Alternatively, try creating a bonnet-bulge – the automotive equivalent of stuffing a sock down the front of your jockeys.

BOOT

If you get a boner when someone mentions 'cubic literage' and think that an estate is what you drive – not where you live – then you're unlikely to be a Boy Racer (the only cubic litres a Boy Racer gets excited about are those under the bonnet).

BOY RACING

Are you a Boy Racer? Take this driving test to find out . . .

1 Someone attempts to overtake you. Do you:

a) Close up the gap with the car in front, so that the offending vehicle has to brake heavily or have a head-on collision with an oncoming vehicle;

b) Begrudgingly let them in, but flash them a few times and give them 'the finger';

c) Slow down slightly to let them in, and then tell yourself that they won't get there any quicker?

2 You notice that a police car is behind you. Do you:

a) Keep an eye on the speedo and drive really carefully;
b) Take the next turning and hope that he won't follow you;
c) Wind down the window to flick a V, nail the pedal to the metal – and then swerve across the road in anticipation of the impending chase?

3 A sporty-looking hatch tears past you on the by-pass, and then slows up – allowing you to overtake – before doing the same thing again. You think that he wants a race. Do you:

a) Follow him at a discreet distance;
b) Slow right down and hope that he'll go away;
c) Change down a gear and chase after him, headlights flashing?

4 A policeman pulls you over for speeding. Do you say to him:

a) 'Is this your ten pound note, Officer?'
b) 'I'm terribly sorry, Sir. It won't happen again. I don't know what came over me.'
c) 'Why aren't you out catching real criminals?'

**5 A cocky pedestrian crossing the road makes
   no effort to speed up when he sees you
   coming. Do you:**

a) Slow down, ever respectful of other road-users;
b) Help his progress by accelerating towards
   him;
c) Scare him by blasting your horn, before passing
   him closely?

**6 A roadhog has taken up residence in the
   middle lane of the motorway – and will not
   move over when the inside lane is clear.
   Annoyed, you:**

a) Overtake him on the inside before cutting him
   up viciously;
b) Move over to the fast lane and pass him
   safely;
c) Tailgate him and flash your headlights until he
   moves over.

**7 You're about to give your drunken mates a lift
   home from the pub when one of them
   suggests you try a 'handbrake turn' in the car
   park. Do you:**

a) Ask what he means;
b) Say that you may do, later, when there aren't
   so many cars around;
c) Charge towards the Beer Garden before jerking
   the wheel and yanking up the handbrake?

8 You lose a wheel-trim. Do you:

a) Order a replacement from the main-dealer;
b) Nick one off a parked car;
c) Use this as an excuse to buy a set of three-spoke alloy wheels, complete with ultra-low profile rubber?

9 Given the choice, you would prefer to read:

a) *Performance Car*;
b) *Max Power*;
c) *Which Campervan*?

10 Your dream car is:

a) A Volvo estate with all the safety features;
b) An Escort Cosworth with a chipped engine;
c) A Mazda MX-5 convertible.

SCORING

1) a-10, b-5, c-0   6) a-10, b-0, c-5
2) a-0, b-5, c-10   7) a-0, b-5, c-10
3) a-5, b-0, c-10   8) a-0, b-5, c-10
4) a-10, b-0, c-5   9) a-5, b-10, c-0
5) a-0, b-10, c-5   10) a-0, b-10, c-5

0–30:
Tartan rug territory. Overly cautious and embarrassingly sensible, you could hardly be tagged a Boy Racer. Emergency application of go-faster paraphernalia to your vehicle may provide a short-

term remedy, but you really should get rid of that Volvo . . .

31–60:
Laddish tendencies are clearly evident, and with their careful cultivation you could certainly enter the higher echelons of Boyracerdom. Try subscribing to Max Power and buying a full-blown bodykit for your hot-hatch.

61–100:
A true Boy Racer. You obviously live for the thrills – and spills – of motoring. Such is your commitment to the cause that you would probably change your name by deed-poll to Kevin and move to Essex. If you weren't already an Essex lad called Kevin, that is.

BRAKES

Dinner plate Tar-oxes are the order of the day here, clamped by multi-pot calipers. If you can't afford them, vent and groove your existing ones with a hammerdrill and a steady hand.

Choose brake pads that are called 'Fast Road' and do f*** all until they're warmed up enough to set your magnesium five-spokes on fire. In the event of brake failure, throw the car into 2nd/1st and ride the car in front – he'll soon brake for you. When desperate, use a bollard or hedge.

BUCKET SEATS

'Buckets' are absolutely essential. Those huggy side-bolsters grip you firmly in corners when you're pulling gs that would make a Tornado pilot pass-out. (As you do in a 1.3 Sport Fiesta.)

The bucket seat is the arch-enemy of the multi-adjustable electric armchair that Shackletons supply to makers of repmobiles.

BUMPER

The effectiveness of a bumper depends upon its construction. The continental shelves that you find strapped to the back of Scandanavian tanks will laugh off nuclear assaults, but most cars are fitted with a fragile chunk of colour-coded plastic which disintegrates at the thought of a proper crunch. Replace it with a spotlight-festooned air dam that can uproot cat's eyes.

BUMPS (and Dents)

These euphemistically describe significant distortions of the bodywork which can't be explained away as 'scratches'. Bumps and dents should normally be blamed on a 'neighbouring vehicle in the car-park', even if a front wing has been caved-in and the collision-ripples finish at the boot.

Of course, panel damage can usually be hammered out (should aesthetics be of prime concern), or alternatively similar damage could be symmetrically duplicated on the opposing flank. You could then claim that the disfigurements are a 'design feature' – or a symbol of having seen action, like WW II pilots who painted kills on their planes.

BUNCHING

Bunching is mass TAILGATING (qv) – an aggressive driving habit frequently practiced by Boy Racers.

When bunching occurs, a group of similarly-suicidal vehicles follow within inches of each other's rear bumpers. Of course, someone has to lead, and more often than not it's a less-than-enthusiastic GRANDAD (qv) who is inconsiderate enough to be doing under-the-ton in the outside lane.

Despite the finely-honed reactions of the Buncher, constant neglect of safety-distances can sometimes result in a fast lane pile-up. To keep your armco-eating chances to a minimum, either get out of the Buncher's way, or try and create some kind of safety-margin behind you. A dab of brake lights (a brake test) may make the car tailing fall-back, but if you are being followed by a hardened Buncher, nothing short of reversing-lights will make him retreat.

BUS

Never being able to pull out seems to mystify drivers. But then they've never had to make the choice between crawling along at 20mph, inhaling diesel fumes and anticipating the next shelter-induced emergency stop – or arriving at their destination on the same day. (Perhaps the Aldwych bus blast was actually an act of terrorism by the Boy Racers Freedom Front.)

C

'Cyclists'

CAR

Comes in many different guises:

- SALOON

Looks like one your Dad's got.
Driven like something out of a Police Stop video by reps.
Goes like cakes in Surbiton.

- SPORTS CAR

Looks like sex on wheels.
Driven like it's late for an accident.
Goes like shit off a shovel.

- COUPÉ

Looks like a saloon in drag.
Driven like a sports car.
Goes like your hairdresser wouldn't believe.

- ESTATE

Looks like a van with windows.
Driven like only Volvo drivers know how.
Goes like it's got three kids and a labrador in the back.

- SHOPPING TROLLEY

Looks like some people are desperate.
Driven like there's a police car behind it.
Goes like you'd expect with a one-point-bugger-all engine.

- HOT HATCH

Looks like a Shopping Trolley on steroids.
Driven like the day after you passed your test.
Goes like Ferrero Rocher at the Ambassador's Reception.

- CONVERTIBLE (CABRIOLET)

Looks like it's raining just after you've put the hood down.
Driven like mad in the Summer.
Goes like a pancake if you roll it.

- TARGA (SPYDER)

Looks like they realised that convertibles leak.
Driven like a coupé most of the time.
Goes like lightning if you leave it overnight in a car park.

CAR BORE

Beware the car bore. You can guarantee that wherever you are, a sad bastard in cords with a goatee and woolly tank-top is gagging to talk to a 'fellow' enthusiast about the trunnions of a Ford Anglia or something equally tragic. Mentioning a topic even vaguely automotive within his earshot will be taken as an invitation for him to join you, 'ginger ale on me'.

Because the car bore is under the delusion that his popularity is directly proportional to the amount of useless motoring trivia recalled in conversation, this monotonous git will talk at you until: a) you slip into a boredom-induced coma; b) you mention football; or c) you lamp him.

CAR GAMES

Kids often play 'car games' in between pissing off their parents by asking when they'll be there. We're talking 'I Spy', 'Animal, Mineral, Vegetable' and number plate spotting. Not to mention that game where you wave at drivers and give them a thumbs-up if they wave back or two-fingers if they don't. That was my favourite.

However, when you move forward a row of seats ten years later, you realise that you can have as much fun in the front:

For starters, there's the Cone Game. The aim is to try and nudge a nominated traffic cone out of line without flattening the whole queue of them. A test of skill and judgment, with only a slight miscalculation separating the powerboat from what you could have won (as Jim Bowen would say).

Then there's the Foot-to-the-Floor Game, where you try and keep the accelerator fully down for as long as possible on the motorway – a test of anticipation and luck (although having a Mini 850 helps).

Alternatively, if you're a member of the local Russian Roulette Drive, you could always time how long you dare keep your eyes shut on the motorway.

CAR WASH

You know it's time to wash the car when you forget what colour it is.

However, washing by hand takes ages, valeting is pricey, and driving your car through an automatic car wash is a humiliating experience – you look like a complete spanner while the machine is in operation (especially if you've left the windows open).

No wonder there are so many filthy motors around bearing the witty request 'clean me'.

CARAVANS

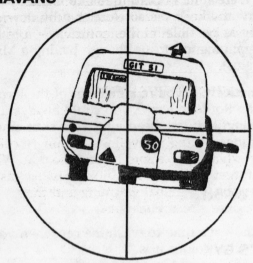

Caravans: Burn nicely.

I just don't understand caravanners. These people *pay money* to be hated by everyone on the roads. They live in plywood sheds. Cook on stoves that take half-an-hour to boil a saucepan of water. And dump in plastic buckets.

It would border on the comprehensible if these wendy-house types couldn't afford to stay in a hotel, but most of them can – judging by their gutbucket Volvos and Granadas.

These bastards must caravan because they want to. Because they actually *enjoy* it.

But enjoy what? The 'freedom' and the 'countryside'?

They'd have more pissing freedom if they weren't towing a bedsit. And the countryside? Bomb-shelter toilet blocks and stand-pipes for scenery. Lovely.

CATALYTIC CONVERTER

Invention that dolphin-huggers jiz over. They think it's sodding marvellous, turning those nasty exhaust gases into carbon dioxide. What they forget is that carbon dioxide is the gas responsible for global warming and the greenhouse effect. Fuckwits.

CAT'S EYE

Reflective stud that scares the shit out of anyone from Bodmin. More famous for the overtold story of its invention than any contribution to road safety.

CATTLE GRID

Tackling cattle grids divides the motoring nation. One school of thought insists that you should crawl over them, letting the suspension carefully readjust between each bar. The other urges high speed negotiation.

Go for the latter. Apparently, it pisses off farmers.

CB RADIOS

All the rage a decade or two ago. People used to call themselves stupid callsigns like 'Mother Duck' and then proceed to talk about 'Smokey' a lot because they'd heard Burt Reynolds say it. The extra-large aerials were needed to counter the electrical interference produced by the user's medallion.

CHASE CAR

The prospect of thrashing a chase car is almost enough to make you want to join the fuzz. Okay, so working in Vice or Narcotics must have their perks, but being obliged to drive a Sierra Cossie at twice the legal limit sounds like a laugh to me.

PIGS CAN FLY

Today's villains are using faster vehicles than ever before. (At least that's what we told the Council when we wanted to have a right old knees-up in some seriously stonking machinery.) Which is why we've got plenty of Cosworths – and even a nice canary yellow M3 – to play with. No holds barred. All at the tax-payers' expense.

Imagine driving a car with:

- blue flashing lights to make you feel very important indeed
- an in-car Vascar camera to record your best chases
- cones in the boot to put anywhere you bloody well like

cont'd overleaf

39

And remember:

- you can pull over decent looking birds and get their name and address by giving them a producer
- red lights and speed limits are 'advisory'
- if you stack it, they'll just bung a few quid on next year's council tax

If you like what you see, fill in the form below and send it to your local police station.

YES! I'd love to cane a Cossie for a living*. And a few hours maxing that Beemer wouldn't go amiss, either. Please give me a job in Traffic.

Name .... Address ....
.... Postcode ....

*I realise that I will actually have to become a police officer to qualify for the 'Drive-a-Cosworth' promotion. And that I'll have to spend 4 years lecturing kids about road safety before even getting into the passenger seat of something quick. In fact, the chances are I'll end up with a Metro like they've got in *The Bill*. (Well, until I become a member of the Masons, at least.)

CHASSIS

Designed for maximum rigidity, the chassis should be strong enough to allow a door to be opened when the car has a single front wheel parked on a kerb.

Although this procedure is a common chassis-strength test, on-lookers might just think that you're crap at parking.

CHIP

A replacement engine management 'brain' that Boy Racers fit to lobotomise their RS Turbos. It gives out a simple instruction – sod the fuel economy and give me more power.

Unfortunately, it also instructs your insurance company that you're a nutter and that cover should be immediately withdrawn.

CLASSIC CAR

Something which Austin Princess Vanden Plas owners think they drive around in, but they don't. Just because something is (thankfully) rare and made before cars had to meet minimum European standards for taste, doesn't mean it should be preserved and labelled 'classic'.

In fact, it gives you a damn good reason for reversing into it at high speed.

CLASSIFIEDS

Small ads used to shift cars, for example:

OPEL MANTA 2.0, 1987, average mileage for year, white, Tts&T'd, lwrd suspension, engine fckd. Thousands spent. First to see will kick tyres before thinking about it. £1995. Tel Phil 0123 432378

SIERRA COSWORTH lookalike, based on piss-slow 1.6L. Looks just like the real thing (car thieves and insurance companies seem to think so, anyway). 1986 D-plate, white, 96 000 miles. One careful lady owner. Before me. Long tax, short MoT. Vented bonnet. Quick sale required due to outstanding debt to local hardman. £895. Tel 0145 765890. Please.

RENAULT 5 GT TURBO G-reg, 65 000 miles, 2000w ICE, only stalls at traffic lights if stereo full volume, white dials, alarm, krbd alloys, Kenwood graphics, deafness forces sale. £3495. Tel 0123 653897 and speak loudly.

CLUTCH

Clutch technique should be as aggressive as possible – especially from a standing start. The only exception is the hill start, when clutch slipping should preside (handbrakes are only for parking and doing a turn in the road).

COACH

Trucks aren't allowed in the fast lane. Coaches are. Work that one out.

However, anyone stuck with hyperactive kids and demented pensioners for three hours can probably be excused racing reps and cutting people up. I'd want to get the journey out of the way myself. And I wouldn't mind making my own entertainment by trying to cause the death of assorted Mondeo drivers, either.

COMMUNICATION

The cabin of a car is an insulated, removed, environment. However, some kind of contact with the outside world can be preserved through communication.

Courtesy gestures, warnings, death threats – these can all be effectively communicated from the driver's seat. If you know how.

Here's a quick guide:

EYE CONTACT

Making eye contact with another driver in heavy traffic – and then smiling – can secure you a place in the queue (the one at the casualty department of a hospital, probably).

HAND SIGNALS

Forget the Highway Code stuff here. You're unlikely to need them as much as the following unofficial variants:

Meaning: The Finger
Made by: Me
Likely recipient: Anyone driving below the national speed limit

Meaning: Wanker
Made by: Simulating masturbation
Likely recipient: People who wear hats in cars

Meaning: The V-sign
Made by: Housewives who reckon it's really insulting
Likely recipient: Some bloke who's just pointed out they shouldn't be on the road

Meaning: Victory
Made by: Newbury by-pass protestors
Likely recipient: Camera crews recording their hippy treehuts being dismantled to make way for a twenty lane super-road

Meaning: Cheers mate
Made by: Sticking your hand up
Likely recipient: Cowards who don't get to the gap first

45

Meaning: Thumbs up
Made by: Freeloading hitch-hiker bastards
Likely recipient: Anything going in the general direction

Meaning: I've spent my student grant on doing up a Beetle
Made by: Bill and Ted types
Likely recipient: Other vee-dubbers at Bug Jams

Meaning: Live long and prosper
Made by: Dr Spock
Likely recipient: Fellow pointy-eared spod

Meaning: The number of the beast
Made by: Teenage heavy-metal fans
Likely recipient: Klüster Bömb's lead guitarist

Meaning: Look at the flashing lights on the roof, sunshine
Made by: Irate coppers
Likely recipient: Speeding Boy Racer

LIGHTS

Lights have always been used to communicate. Here's a summary of today's signals:

LIGHT SIGNAL	MEANING
Left/Right Indicator	*I am not a minicab driver.*
Right Indicator (used in the fast lane)	*Move over, you twat.*
Full-beam flash	<u>Official Highway Code meaning</u> *I'm here.* <u>Unofficial meaning</u> *Depends on situation. Could be anything from 'After you' to 'F*** you'.*
Multiple flashes	*Pray that the next light's green.*
Headlights or foglights on for no reason	*I drive a Volvo.*
Hazard lights	**a)** *I've broken down.* **b)** *I'm braking heavily.* **c)** *I've just popped into the shops. I won't be five minutes. Honest.*

HORN

Used like a full-beam flash, but in situations where the headlights would be useless (expert tailgating).

It is illegal to sound the horn after eleven at night, although shagging couples in steamed-up cars should always be given some laddish encouragement.

CONCEPT CAR

A one-off styling exercise penned by a frustrated designer who has spent the past five years designing door handles. Helps keep studio staff from topping themselves and gives motoring journos something to get wet about.

CONES, TRAFFIC

Traffic cones are a great British institution. You'll see millions in your lifetime – if you travel on motorways or visit a lot of student bedrooms.

Acres of orange plastic that don't cordon off any roadworks can be explained by the fact that it is cheaper to store cones on a motorway than in a DoT warehouse.

COOKING

If a dealer tells you that a car is a 'cooking' model don't expect to find a stove in the boot.

The 'cooking' version is the most basic, ordinary, bottom-of-the-shit-pile standard vehicle. Which probably means that the passenger's door – let alone airbag – is an optional extra.

CORNERS

Trickier than straights, these. You should be aware of the following:

- THE KINK. Slight bend in the road – not really a corner at all.
- THE Z-BEND/S-BEND. Should be taken as fast as possible, preferably tail-out. (If you want to die.)
- THE U-BEND. Logical name for a hairpin. Especially considering the fact that you'd be up shit creek if you got it wrong.
- THE SWEEPER. A long, sweeping corner. Surprisingly.

CRASH

There are some things you just don't want to crash into. A tanker covered in lots of diamond-shaped markings. A police car. A Volvo.
See ACCIDENTS.

CRUISE

Modified-car owners convention. All feature:

- A bloke in a Capri doing doughnuts to the delight of the gathered crowd;
- Even the saddest git in his Mum's Astra 1.4 spinning the wheels down to the beading;
- Birds. (Who hide in the cars away from all the mooning).

Tradition has it that the bizzies turn up just before the sound-off causes structural damage to the Borough of Dagenham, and give a producer to anything with a pulse.

CRUISE CONTROL

Worth a mention, because it's always fun to see how long you can keep the system set on a motorway journey – a less demanding variation of the Foot to the Floor CAR GAME (qv).

Alternatively, if you're the passenger in a car equipped with this device, setting it without the driver knowing will give him the shock of his life when he lifts off and the car doesn't slow down. Probably not one for a rush-hour M25, though.

CUT AND SHUT

What's this problem Roger Cook has with cut and shut cars? Two cars for the price of one? Sounds like a good deal to me. Okay, so you probably wouldn't want to get the bastard involved with an artic, but then I know people who think that's what he deserves.

CUTTING-UP

The staple Boy Racing manoeuvre. Easy to execute – simply pull in front of a car you've just passed (nearly taking its front off). If the car behind has been cut-up proficiently, flashed reprisals should be below your boot-line – and therefore out-of-sight.

CYCLISTS

Motorists rationally dislike a few certain types of pedaller. This animosity is normally shown by passing the cyclist at a destabilising speed – or by swerving/shouting at the two-wheeled git when alongside.

Those detested include:

a) The Roadhog Racer. Who always insists on cycling abreast of his partner, taking up as much tarmac as possible. Obviously forgets that he doesn't pay road tax.

b) The Weaver. A particularly annoying cyclist who seems to have lost all sense of balance and co-ordination. Pedals his Grifter standing-up, drifting and correcting continuously. One handed or no-handed steering is common.

c) The Eco-Cyclist. Who believes that cycling is the only morally acceptable form of transport and that cars are the machinery of Beelzebub. Frequently casts contemptuous, self-righteous glances towards drivers – from behind a Chernobyl issue smog mask.

D

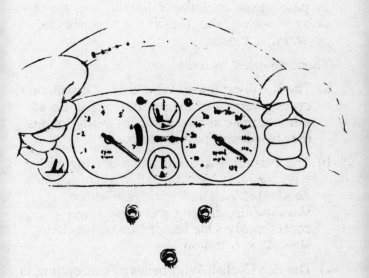

'Dashboard'

DAISIES, PUSHING UP

See CRASHES INVOLVING ONCOMING
JUGGERNAUTS

DASHBOARD

That plank of plastic behind the steering wheel.

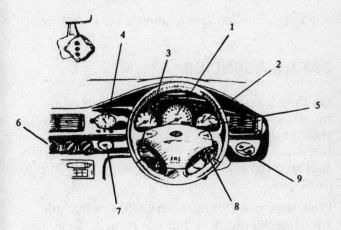

1 Speedo (over-reads to impress your mates)
Odometer (funny how the numbers don't line
up)

2 Fuel gauge (sinks slowly to start with, then
drops like a rock)

3 Revcounter (lets you know how much fun your car's having)

4 Clock (tells correct time. In China)

5 Water temperature gauge (saves you having to dip an elbow)

6 Heating controls (by Fisher-Price)

7 Heated rear window (handwarmer in Skodas)

8 Porsche key-ring (to flash at nightclubs)

9 Foglight switch (permanently on in Volvos)

DATING AGENCIES

Do they take the piss or what? Month after month, car magazines carry ads about 'meeting your perfect partner' and 'finding true love'. Introduction agencies must think they've captured the market for sad, lonely people who can't pull.

Well, they can f*** off with their wanky little anecdotes about how Bill got on with Jane. I can pull – without using (much) pheremone spray, and don't want to fill in an irrelevant form about 'which word describes me best.'

Desperateline

Herbert and Samantha

Complete this questionnaire now. The sooner you fill in this form on behalf of your mate, the sooner you can make his life a misery.

Personal Information
Name:
Name the local kids call you:
Marital Status:
☐ Single
☐ Divorced
☐ Playing Around
Age:
Real age:
Pretend occupation:
Weird religion:

Education
☐ Woodwork Prize in Second Year
☐ Open University
☐ Science Programmes with Carol Vorderman

Your Personality
- [ ] Sad
- [ ] Beyond sad
- [ ] Shy
- [ ] Sinister
- [ ] Split

Your Interests
- [ ] Trainspotting
- [ ] Amateur radio
- [ ] Frightening children
- [ ] Wearing half-mast flares
- [ ] Washing infrequently
- [ ] Tennents Super
- [ ] Folk music
- [ ] Killing animals
- [ ] Talking to yourself

Details of the partner you would like
- [ ] Swedish
- [ ] Blonde
- [ ] Legs up to armpits
- [ ] Goes like a BR 6350 Tractor Unit

Please complete this form and return it to us today. You will then receive in the strictest confidence:

1. Embarrassing follow-up correspondence
2. The name and brief description of someone who could be your perfect victim, er partner
3. Junk mail for eternity

DESIGN, AUTOMOTIVE

Car styling is a slave to fashion. If curves are 'in' expect blancmange-like efforts to escape from automotive design houses. If they're not, and angular styling is the vogue, origami creations will prevail. Driving the wrong shape for the current trend is virtually admitting to a collection of bri-nylon shirts with hang-glider collars – although you can take the bus safe in the knowledge that fashion is cyclical and that one day you'll be able to take your car out of the garage without shame.

DRAGSTER

300mph machine designed to eat up quarter-mile strips as quickly as possible.

Unfortunately, the apocalyptical image created by two thousand horsepower and nitrous injection is severely compromised by those two bicycle wheels at the front.

DRINK DRIVING

After ten pints of lager your reasoning lapses and overwhelming self-confidence surges through your being. Take on that brick-hard psycho in the corner? No problem. Pull that beautiful bird at the bar? Easy.

Behind the wheel there's overtaking on blind corners and handbrake turns on the motorway.

So think what you'd be like if you were pissed.

THE BOY RACER'S HANDBOOK BAG-FREE BOOZE TEST
Is the person sitting next to you:
a) male
b) female
c) your beshtesht friend in the whole world ever.

Scoring: a) pass b) pass c) fail.

DRIVER

Drivers fall into different types – the Boy Racer and the Grandad spring immediately to mind, but these aren't the only ones. There are a few others which should be instantly recognisable to the perceptive road-user:

The BACKSEAT DRIVER, for example, is unmistakable – 'Don't overtake. It's OK to go now. Are you in the right gear? Slow down!' . . .

If backseat driving is too intrusive, try turning up the stereo – although many culprits sensibly suggest that you should stop the car and let them walk.

SUNDAY DRIVERS are nearly as infuriating. Emerging from their secure accommodation on Sundays and Bank Holidays, Sunday Drivers are the scourge of the highways. Attracted to areas of 'scenic beauty', the four-wheeled day-tripper painfully demonstrates the fact that he drives only one day a week. The worst type of Grandad.

THE POSEUR wears sun-glasses all the time, even at night, which is why he's got a Braille speedo fitted. All mirrors are angled so that he can check his hair whichever way he looks, and a tub of hair gel is often found in the glove compartment. Favours white cars, especially convertibles.

THE REP. Covers 100 000 motorway miles a year, all at 3ft from the car in front. Highly experienced . . . at cutting people up and tailgating. Specification obsessed (the 'i's have it). Jacket often seen hanging in the rear side window.

(Interestingly, manufacturer's performance figures are frequently obtained by reps, such is their extraordinary ability to extract the last few mph out of a 2-litre Cavalier.)

DRIVETRAIN

What every boy wants to do when he grows up.

DUAL CARRIAGEWAY

Fast two-laned roads which bring out the Boy Racer in even the most sensible pensioner. Frequent 'cat and mouse' antics suggest that the label 'Duel Carriageway' would be more appropriate.

Supposedly policed less than motorways, but that must be bollocks because I got an SP30 on one last year.

E

'Exhaust'

ELECTRIC

Not only is this the name of countless crappy LIMITED EDITIONS (qv), but the type of vehicle pundits reckon we'll all be driving in the year 2010. Well, I want my car to sound like a car, not a *fridge*. And I want it to go like a car, too. Not crawl around the place at 5 mph like one of those spacky milk floats. Moulinex GTi? F*** off.

EMERGENCY STOP

The only conceivable reason why you would want to take your driving test in a G-reg Fiesta.

ENGINE

It should be noted that 'Suck, Squeeze, Bang, Blow' refers to the firing cycle of a four-stroke internal combustion engine, not the options available in a Thailand massage parlour (as far as I know).

The more cc it's got the bigger your reputation and thus, to all your mates anyway, the bigger your dick.

For ultimate Boy Racer cred you need as many bhp under the bonnet as possible. For best results put a 9-litre Mack engine into a Nova.

Should still be room for one passenger (before the ICE).

ESSEX

The spiritual home of Boy Racing. Where you turn off the lights before a shag by closing the car door.

EVEL KNIEVEL

The only stuntman to have a road sign designed in his honour.

EXHAUST

The more powerful a car, the more exhaust pipes it tends to have sticking out the back (see FAST CAR RATIO). Therefore, Boy Racers should be aware of the 'one-into-two' tail-pipe trim – which may fool the unsuspecting into thinking you've got a fast car, not a Ford Fiesta Popular*.

*Sorry. That just isn't true. People will think you are extremely sad and laugh at you loudly. A Ford Fiesta Popular is – and always will be – a Ford Fiesta Popular. Even if you stick a 500 horse Cosworth engine in it. ('Popular' means 'shopping' in any language.)

F

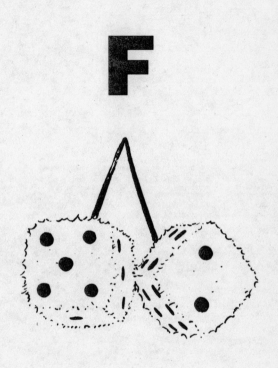

'Fluffy Dice'

FAN

Electrical component that does what the f*** it wants to, regardless of whether the car's running or not. Cheeky bastard.

FASHION

Typical driving attire of Boy Racer

Headwear: Baseball cap (reversed)
Eyewear: Sunglasses (preferably mirrored)
Jewellery: St Christopher gold chain
Smalls: Briefs
Favourite accessory: Socks to go down briefs
Favourite outfit: T-shirt and shellsuit
Shoes: White Reeboks

Typical driving attire of Grandad

Headwear: Flat cap (tweed)
Eyewear: Bi-focal binoculars
Jewellery: Pacemaker
Smalls: Y-fronts
Favourite accessory: Incontinence pads to go down
  Y-fronts
Favourite outfit: Cardigan and corduroy
Shoes: Carpet slippers

FAST CAR RATIO

The Fast Car Ratio was a childhood system
designed to assess the desirability of a car. It
worked on the naive premise that fast cars had

lots of exhaust pipes and very few windscreen wipers. Therefore, the formula was as follows:

$$\text{FAST CAR RATIO (fcr)} = \frac{\text{Number of exhaust pipes}}{\text{Number of windscreen wipers}}$$

This meant that the Lamborghini Countach – a supercar of enormous pre-pubescent admiration – attained a score of 4 (four exhausts divided by one wiper), and your Dad's estate scored a catastrophic $1/3$ (a sole exhaust divided by two front wipers and the one at the back).

Analysis indicated that Argos was therefore 12 times more likely to market a Lambo alarm clock and duvet cover set than a Montego Countryman one.

FINES

Those weekly instalments you've been paying to the magistrate's court for the past three years.

FLASHING

See COMMUNICATION or your local park.

FLUFFY DICE

Laddish icon. Nothing symbolises Boy Racing better than a pair of fluffy dice gently swinging to the lilt of lateral forces, warmly obscuring your vision and cheekily distracting you. Not even a wide-arch Astra with twin-headlamp conversion.

Supposedly a lucky mascot, with each pair of opposite sides adding up to that mythical number of fortune, seven. (But if you believe that you probably think David Icke is the Son of God, not just a weird ex-goalie who used to be on TV).

DICE ADVICE

- Comb regularly
- Hand wash only
- Keep away from compulsive gamblers

FOUR-WHEEL DRIVE

Personally, I grew out of Tonka trucks at least a decade ago, but if people want to embarrass themselves in off-road machinery then that's fine by me. It's a free country.

WORST 4×4 OFFENDERS:

1. *The city-based wanker in a Range Rover.* Wears Barbour over suit. Thinks the 'diff lock' is a security feature.
   Goes off-road only when it's necessary to park on the pavement.

2. *Disco kid and his Vitara.* Poseur. Loves bullbars and chromed three-spokes.
   Goes off-road if there's a rave in a field.

3. *The rustic duffer with a battered Land Rover.* Senile old farmer who takes to the road occasionally. Sheepdog in back of prehistoric Landie.
   Goes off-road evidently not enough.

FUEL

Numerous types are available:

PETROL   Comes in various grades and configurations. Leaded four-star the most potent straight-from-the-pump jungle juice, but now superseded by the more ecological unleaded stuff, which is a bit poofier. Two-star now extinct, which is fair enough because it was a waste of time anyway. (Only idiots put it in anything other than a lawnmower. Like tramps who used to fill their hip-flasks with it.) Some petrol now includes detergent, which probably makes Nanette Newman happier.

DIESEL Originally the diet of trucks only, but a few years back some tight git worked out that you could reduce running costs by using it in cars. However, the cars were more expensive than the petrol ones – so you had to drive 100 000 miles before breaking even. And your car sounded like a tractor.

METHANOL Isn't available at your local filling station – although NASA will probably sell you some. If your car runs off this you either own a dragster or a very disturbed mind.

NITROUS OXIDE Is similarly explosive, but is mixed with petrol whilst on the move. The injection process begins with a press of the skull-and-crossboned button hidden in your gearstick and ends when your engine grenades at 9000 revs. Neck-snapping acceleration guaranteed.

PEANUT BUTTER Car manufacturers have the technology to produce cars which run off virtually anything. Cooking oil and peanut butter are just two of the possible fuels. Not as absurd a scheme as it seems, as filling your car up with peanut butter can only be better than eating it.

G

'Gears . . . Dog-Leg First'

GARAGE

Garages come in two types – Commercial and Domestic:

COMMERCIAL GARAGES

- Filling Stations. Petrol pumps mere formality. Main business is flogging tampons and Johnny Cash cassettes (a reaction to supermarkets selling fuel). Long queue of students buying cigarettes and crisps after midnight.
- Car Showrooms. Ceiling-to-floor glass, strategic aspidistra, marooned desk, distinctive 'new car' aroma. Yet to diversify into baby food and flowers.

DOMESTIC GARAGES

Compete with the tip, not Sainsbury's.
Each should include the following:

- a jam jar full of tepid turps
- a cobweb in the corner that you're secretly afraid of
- various power tools of industrial specification to mark your territory

GATSO

The Gatso speed camera is a pain in the Boy Racer's arse. Any greedy council with a couple of half-decent driving roads now has a fleet of them. But they can be beaten.

For a start, the humble radar detector should tell you whether the grey box is armed or not. And then flash-reflective number plates or a radar interceptor may provide a bit of protection if it is packing Kodak.

However, the use of these systems is about as legal as marrying your sister, so what other tricks are there?

Some comfort can be gained from the fact that half the cameras are decoys, and that the rest only tend to go off in serious cases. Red lights have to be jumped blatantly and speed limits broken conclusively for that double flash to indicate that you've been done.

Boy Racers may also be glad to know that the Gatso won't operate if two cars break the beam in close convoy. High speed tailgating has never been so beneficial!

GEARS

MANUAL gears. Invented to keep the unco-ordinated off the roads. Effective until automatics came along.

AUTOMATIC gearboxes are fitted to cars driven
by people who are either:
a) extremely lazy;
b) very thick because they can't master manual
   gears
c) arthritic – especially in that right ankle.

SEMI-AUTOMATIC gears combine the best
aspects of manual and automatic systems.
Some types use F1-style buttons to go up and
down the box while others retain the gearstick
– but all get rid of the thigh-flexing clutch, and
should therefore be left for the ladies.

GLOVE COMPARTMENT

Fancy name for a horizontal bin.

GRANDAD

The antithesis of the Boy Racer. Wears patterned
socks, brown polyester (or corduroy) trousers
and drives a 'cooking' family saloon/hatch.

Grandads can normally be identified from a
distance by their choice of car colour. Any shade
of brown (especially cream) should immediately
arouse suspicion – and so should most blues.
Orange, and other hues that warrant a large
discount from a dealer, are also Grandad
colours.

The Grandad is often a bit infirm and is likely to suffer from a rheumatoid right foot – which is why he can be found doing 45 on the motorway. His driving is laboured and incompetent, and his ability to hog the road is second only to his habit of making sudden changes of direction without indicating.

If the car and style of driving don't enable recognition at 500 yards, close inspection of the suspect vehicle is bound to yield the truth. Look out for:

- THE TARTAN RUG. Always a dead give away. Invariably found on the rear passenger seat.
- THE BOX OF TISSUES. Positioned on the rear shelf. Needed to mop up after Ethel's little accidents.
- SUN-BLINDS. Stuck on the rear window. Grandads might be able to see the traffic held up behind them if they didn't have these down all the time.
- BOILED SWEETS. False-teeth-friendly tinned confectionery can normally be found in the glove compartment.
- SCENTED WIPES. Also found in the glove compartment. Something to do with Ethel again, I imagine.

GTi

The definitive hot hatch badge. Rarer now that silly insurance premiums have forced manufacturers to tone-down their faster machines (the next Ford Cosworth, for example, will be called the Ford Countryman TDXSi and come in estate form only).

Don't let anything put you off a GTi, though. They might be expensive to insure, easy to crash and a joy to steal – but they look good, go better and modify the best. Get a GTi. Sod the GiTs.

GUEST, JOANNE

Fit bird who takes her kit off for readers of laddish motoring mags. Rated as the most fanciable lust object after a Peco big bore exhaust by the readership of *Fast Car*.

H

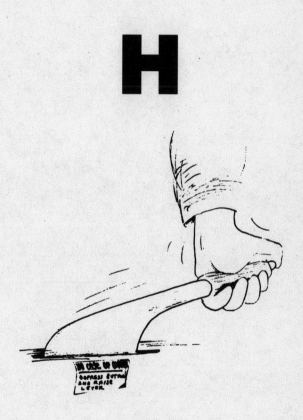

IN CASE OF DOUBT
DEPRESS EXTRA
AND RAISE
LEVER

'Handbrake'

HAIRDRESSER'S CAR

As sure as a boxer drives a black Merc with tinted windows, the hairdresser tarts around the place in an oriental sports car. The top hairdresser's cars are outed below:

1. **NISSAN 200SX**. Unisex coupé that looks a bit like a salon, sorry, saloon. Powerful and rear wheel drive, but so forgiving even the shampoo girl could handle it.
Verdict: The Nissan 200 ESSEX.

2. **MAZDA MX-5**. Open-topped, so you can let your mop blow dry. Coiffured good looks. Poor value considering pansy performance.
Verdict: Hardly a snip, but cuts a dash.

3. **TOYOTA MR2**. Gervaise reckons it looks a bit like a Ferrari, but that sounds like a pony tale to me. Mid-engined, with short back and sides.
Verdict: Camp champ.

HANDBRAKE

Every Boy Racer knows that the handbrake is used for parking – but that its principal application is for initiating the handbrake turn (known by Saga-subscribers as a 'bootlegger turn').

This manoeuvre is the ultimate 'turn in the road'. Forget forward and reverse gears – just hit 30mph, depress the clutch, flick on some lock, and yank up the handbrake.

Easy.

Of course, you'd better make sure that the handbrake operates the rear wheels – because you'd look a complete nugget if the front wheels were connected.

HANDLING

The handling of a car depends on the type of transmission.

FRONT-WHEEL DRIVE cars tend to understeer when cornering hard, sending the nose arcing into the undergrowth.

REAR-WHEEL DRIVE endows a vehicle with the more exciting habit of oversteer, whereby the back steps out of line – possibly resulting in a SPIN (qv).
Again, you risk eating hedge.

FOUR-WHEEL DRIVE on the other hand, blesses a car with a very mild slide when grip is lost. The rear end stands about as much chance of swapping with the front as with a pantomime horse.

HIGHWAY CODE

The HMSO Highway Code is a bit like one of those secret documents you see on Mission Impossible. Read it once (the night before the

driving test) and then forget it soon after.
Eating it is optional (mine tasted quite nice).

HIRE-PURCHASE AGREEMENT

The only thing on your car that will last forever.

Sample

Ford Escort RS2000

Cash price: £14995

Deposit: £5000 and your grandmother

Balance: £9995

Daily repayments: 2135 × £168.79

Total repayments: £456734

APR (All Possession Risked) =

13.8 % pa (per afternoon)

Acme Finance Ltd is an unlicenced credit broker.
All loans subject to status and what we can get
away with. Failure to keep up with payments could
put your kneecaps at risk.

HORN

Used for COMMUNICATION (qv) and also to
scare horses (see ANIMALS).

HOT ROD

Dragster in drag. Owners grow beards to convince themselves that liking crushed velvet upholstery isn't actually admitting to homosexuality.

HOTTING

Slang term for hotwiring. Kids these days couldn't change a lightbulb, but give them the loom of an XR2 and they'd have it rewired backwards within five minutes.

To test the theory, leave a locked-up hot hatch in a Liverpool housing estate next to a midi-system without a plug. A tenner says the car goes first.

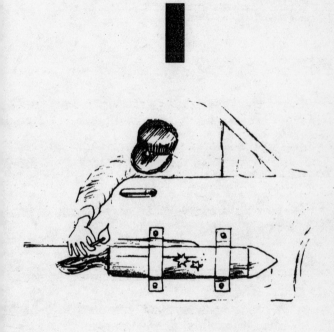

'Ignition'

ICE

ICE: Leaves you shaken and stirred

In Car Entertainment. And we're not talking
about pissy auto-reverse upgrades for your
Goldstar. We're talking the full monty –
crossovers, bass tubes and subwoofers. Stuff
that would make your Gran run to her
Andersen shelter.

The head unit's the nerve centre of the system.
Lots of twiddly bits and a display panel. Four
huge amps and a ninety-disc CD changer in the
boot ensure that your shopping can look
elsewhere for a ride. Jodrell Bank subwoofers
and Channel Tunnel bass tubes provide
Mr Richter with something to measure, while
tweeters do the business at the top end.
Crossovers sort it all out.

IGNITION

Ignition is normally initiated by a key, but
HOTTING (qv) has the same effect. Boy Racers
should always prod the throttle to try and catch
the engine when starting-up – and give the
accelerator an enthusiastic blip just before
turning-off, too.

INCHING

A curious act practised by Boy Racers at traffic
lights. Combining machismo with impatience,
the Boy Racer will move his car forward inch
by inch in eager anticipation of the lights
changing. Invariably, this means that he is a
great deal over the white line (in fact, may even
have reached the other side of the junction) by
the time the lights do actually give the signal
to go ahead.

Inching is the product of a fallible intuition
(which tells the Boy Racer when the lights will
change) and a simple straining-at-the-leash
urge. Its main function, of course, is to gain an
advantage of a few yards when setting-off from
the lights. By doing this – and edging in front
of any driver parallel to him – the Boy Racer is
proclaiming his masculinity. Obviously, this
tends to incite other drivers (especially fellow
Boy Racers) to inch forward themselves,
leading to an inching competition.

INSTRUMENTS

COOKING (qv) cars are renowned for their lack of instrumentation. Cost-cutting measures include leaving out the rev counter (a heinous crime) and replacing the space with a clock (not that you'd notice – the tacho needle would take a minute to go round anyway).

Digital instruments never caught on – despite the popularity of *Knightrider* (possibly because people were worried that the car would come with a gay-sounding voice, too) – but white-faced dials are becoming increasingly popular.

INSURANCE

Insurance companies would rather honour a claim than give cover to a driver who is:
a) young; b) accident-prone; or c) convicted.

Boy Racers are often all three.

Therefore, to dissuade anyone who doesn't live in a rest home from taking out insurance with them, firms impose discouraging premiums and excesses* (perhaps even refusing cover at any price).

Short of filling in the form fraudulently by 'forgetting' to include the last couple of accidents, 'absent-mindedly' missing out the eight speeding convictions, or claiming to be a subscriber to *Readers Digest*, the Boy Racer is resigned to policy persecution until he has a no-claims bonus as long as his arm and the Austin Allegro to match.

*Be suspicious if they don't. The lower the premium, the more elaborate the excuse for not paying out.

INTERCOOLER

Bit in turbocharged cars that cools the inter.

J

'Joyriding'

J-TURN

A bit like a handbrake turn in reverse. But
without the handbrake. Just whack on some
lock and dab the brakes when you're doing
30 mph backwards.

JOYRIDING

AN IDIOT'S GUIDE TO JOYRIDING

1. Wait for children's television to end.
2. Find a Y-reg Escort XR3.
3. Break in, smash steering lock and hotwire.
4. Move seat all the way forward in order to reach
   pedals.
5. Drive around local housing estate. Attract
   bizzies' attention by wheelspinning and doing
   handbrake turns.
6. Invite fuzz to follow by throwing empty rusk
   packets at them.
7. Crash and burn car. Go home to bed.

JUMP STARTING

More fun than a lights-on buzzer.

K

'Kamikaze'

KARTING

When I spend £15 for ten minutes on a kart track, I don't want some twat telling me not to use the brake and accelerator at the same time, or that I'll be hauled in for bumping my mates. I'll do what the f*** I want. If I want to drive backwards or shag the centrifugal clutch, then I shall. *Fifteen notes*. What does that cover? A bit of petrol and rent of a helmet that smells of a hospital, that's what. You could rebuild the buggers for a couple of Ayrtons.

KAMIKAZE

The death-wish driver who gambles with his life every journey. Drivers of the Divine Wind overtake on blind bends, race down single-track country roads and jump traffic lights compulsively.

Rising Sun bandana is optional, washable brown seat covers are not.

KERBING

Scuffing your alloy wheel whilst trying to run over a pedestrian.

KEVS, THE

Forget the Oscars. Forget the BAFTAS and the
BRITS. The KEVS are the awards that matter.
Stacking your car spectacularly or getting
banned might be cause for nomination, but to
pick up one of these little beauties you really
need to make an outstanding contribution to
the Boy Racing cause. Just look at the roll of
honour below.

BEN HUR
*Ancient Roman chariot racer who found out that
being the fastest bloke around made you very popular. However, all the girls and glory have to be
put in perspective – two horsepower just isn't that
impressive . . .*
Award: Posthumous Kev

CAPTAIN SMITH OF THE TITANIC
*Trying to handbrake turn an ocean liner gets my
respect. And that iceberg could have happened to
anybody. Pure bloody bad luck, if you ask me.
Further respect for having gone down with most of
the female passengers.*
Award: Posthumous Kev

THE CAMPBELLS
*Dad Malcolm set a pre-war land speed record. Son
Donald topped himself at 300 mph in a speedboat
attempting to meet Norris McWhirter. Top lads.*
Awards: Posthumous Kevs for them both

JAMES DEAN

Rebel without a cause – unless you count Boy Racing. Won a game of chicken on screen, but wasn't so lucky in real life – becoming a rebel without a pulse when he totalled his hairdressery Porsche Speedster.

Award: Posthumous Kev

GILLES VILLENEUVE

Grand Prix hero bloke from Canada. Drove every-where ten-tenths – even when he was out to collect a pint of milk rather than a podium position. Stalled helicopters for a laugh. Died a true Boy Racer trying to overtake a slower car.

Award: Posthumous Kev

KIT CAR

There are two kit car nightmare scenarios:

You realise that the bits don't fit together as well as they do in the Instruction Manual photographs – and that you're not the torque-wrench wielding Meccano-fetishist that you thought you were. You sell the project as '95% complete, all parts to finish' and buy something constructed by a robot.

or

As soon as you have built half of it, you realise that some bits are missing, vital for completion. You ring up the manufacturer. He says that the parts are yet to be designed and that he'll call you when they're ready. Four months later you ring up again. All you get is an answerphone saying that the company is in receivership. You sell the project to an unsuspecting punter as '95% complete, all parts to finish' . . .

'Level Crossings . . .'

LANE DISCIPLINE

There are two golden rules.

Give way to faster machinery. Respect should always be given to anything quicker than you. Or anything that looks quicker than you. This means that a McLaren F1 cacks itself when an XR3i with full Rieger F40 bodykit comes up behind it.

Ignore slower stuff trying to get past. Lesser vehicles can piss up a rope if they think you're going to move over. They've got as much right to flash and tailgate as you have to brake test them.

LEARNING

Learners: Social outcasts (like all Micra drivers).

Everyone hates learners – but there's nothing wrong with that. It's good for them. Where would be the incentive to pass the test if it wasn't for other road-users thinking that you're a wanker and treating you like you've just pissed in the shallow-end?

Once the L-plates are off, though, you can start to dish out some of the same. That swift role reversal means that you can be a bastard to School of Motoring Corsas, getting right up behind them on hill starts and trying to make them crash at junctions by sounding your two-tone impatiently. Unless you've got green L-plates on, which is like trying to convince everyone that your leprosy has cleared up.

You can also forget everything that you've learnt, crash and get done for speeding – but only if you want to feel like you really belong.

LEVEL CROSSINGS, BIT IN THE HIGHWAY CODE ABOUT

The only part of The Highway Code that interests people*, as it details what you should do if your car breaks down on a level crossing.

*except Volvo drivers, who aren't scared of anything. In fact, it's train drivers who worry (see VOLVO ON THE LINE, BIT IN THE RAILWAY CODE ABOUT).

LIFTS

Most people who give lifts to their mates get taken for granted at some stage. Tell-tale signs include:
– Passengers climbing straight into the back;

- being tipped;
- friends hailing you in the street.

LIMITED EDITION

Trick used by manufacturers to get rid of oddly-coloured cars that no-one wants.

After adding some 'special equipment' (a pop-up sunroof and a pair of trimmed headrests), on go the twatty decals. The resulting travesty is then given a name that sounds exotic to people who live on the Isle of Wight – 'Mango' or 'St Tropez' or something – and then launched amidst a blaze of publicity.

The bird in the advert is normally quite shaggable but a greedy bitch who complains that she didn't get a free car like the stick-insect who does the rival ads.

LO-RIDERS

Sad American shit favoured by people who reckon that it's still cool to dress like Mr T and say 'man' a lot. What's even more tragic is that they think a car moving with the grace and co-ordination of a mad cow has street cred. Save your money for some Bilsteins, boys.

LORRY

Lorries do what they want on the road – because they're bigger. A lorry pulling out in front of you without looking doesn't give a flying one. If there's a collision he's not going to be involved, six feet in the air behind his collection of triangular flags.

Lorries always flash each other, too. When one truck has eventually got past the lorry it has spent ten minutes overtaking, the overtaken truckie will give his mate a wink-wink nudge-nudge full-beam blast of his headlights. This is a congratulatory move, praising the other lorry driver for taking so long over the manoeuvre. The traffic behind will have been successfully held up because of this dazzling display of teamwork (it's a well known fact that lorry drivers hate everyone else on the road).

Some people (who play the saddest game in the world – Haulage Company Vehicle Spotting) actually enjoy looking out for lorries – and not just the ones that are about to kill them.

LSD

LSD: Beats the breathalyser.

Getting into the car with someone who swears
by the effects of an LSD can be dodgy. He either
takes a tab of acid before setting off, or believes
in the benefits to traction that a limited slip
differential can provide. Make sure you find out
which before setting off. If there's any hint of
stifled wheelspin, forget it. You'll be in for a
boring ride.

M

'Magazines'

MAGAZINE

Motoring titles are always placed on the shelf below the soft porn in newsagents. This geography occurs because of a similarity in subject-matter – detailed photographs of models that blokes would like to get inside.

MANOEUVRE

To piss about at slow speed (see GRANDAD).

MIRRORS

Checked more regularly than the view ahead by studious learners (on the pretext of 'safety'). Also checked by Poseurs (see DRIVER) who worry about their parting – and police-wary Boy Racers who worry about *their* parting (with their licences).

'Mirror Signal Manoeuvre' is the classic driving scheme, but many drivers have simplified this rather cumbersome procedure. Instead of 'MSM', the new system is contracted to the last 'M'.

MOMENT

Near accident. Ensures that the self-preserving never ask you for a lift again.

MOPED

see SAD, VERY

MOT

Every car over three years old has to have an annual roadworthiness check. The test can be all the more difficult to pass if your motor is completely shot or if the garage doesn't take bribes.

MOTORBIKE

Motorbikes aren't as inherently annoying as bicycles, but they can still get on your tits – especially by cruising smugly past when you're in a traffic jam. Changing lanes as often as possible keeps them on their toes.

You'll probably meet a nutter on a superbike at the lights sometime. He'll fancy his chances, but carefully aimed washer nozzles are a good distraction.

MOTORSPORT

Boy Racing under controlled conditions. See examples below:

CIRCUIT RACING

This takes place on a racing track. Look out for such features as the pits, the paddock and the bridge that looks like half a tyre. Like the M25, all types of machinery circulate a tarmac loop in the heat of competition.

Winner the first car driven over the start/finish line.

STOCK CAR RACING

Cheap circuit racing. Demolition Derby a real crowd pleaser (probably something to do with seeing all those Cortinas getting stacked).

Winner the only car capable of being driven over the start/finish line.

AUTOTESTS

Parking against the clock. Irrelevant when you consider that motorway roadworks often allow you to weave around cones at 80 mph anyway.

HILLCLIMBING

Getting up a hill in as little time as possible.

TRIALS

Getting up a hill.

RALLYING

One of the most realistic forms of motorsport, with competitors allowed a passenger to egg them on. Made more exciting by the proximity of cagouled spectators to the action.

MOTORWAY

High speed road consisting of three lanes and a hard shoulder – an 'emergency' lane used by Boy Racers if there is stationary traffic in the other three.

N

'Nitrous Oxide'

NITROUS OXIDE

Fuel additive causing four-stroke hyperactivity (see FUEL). Also used as an anaesthetic during childbirth, which could explain a few things.

NOUGHT-TO-SIXTY

Crucial performance statistic governing standing start acceleration. Anything that takes over ten seconds is probably registered in Eastbourne.

Figures are normally obtained by a roadtester with a licence to fry clutches and turn treads into slicks, so make sure you've got a mate at Kwik-fit before attempting to repeat them. Milliseconds can be shaved off the time by running an empty tank of fuel, kicking out the passengers and having a dump.

NUMBER PLATE

Boy Racers choose non-standard lettering for their plates as it baffles the bloke trying to decipher the Gatso film. As does making an antisocial word out of your reg (M1 NGE, PEN 15 etc.).

Toffs' plates with meaningless initials get no respect.

'Overcook'

OIL

There are many different types of oil available so choose carefully (don't put cooking oil in your car just because it happens to be 'cooking').

As a general rule, go for something with a sillier name than what you drive. (QX might do for a GL, but your GTi needs ZRQ-Xtralube at the very least.)

OPPOSITE LOCK

Turning into a tail-slide is a situation most Boy Racers relish. Skid pans, deserted car parks and busy roundabouts are used to perfect this technique.

OVERCOOK

To wipe-out. Like the culinary equivalent, the result is normally a soft, mushy mess that has to be scraped up. (Except this time it's you, not your dinner.)

OVERTAKING

Boy Racers cannot blame their suicidal overtaking moves on impatience or courage – the problem lies with the large number of vehicles which beg to be overtaken no matter what. These 'overtakable' vehicles need religious self-control to stay behind.

The culprits are:

The Austin Rover Maestro

Strongly associated with Grandads and likely to be driven slowly. Tartan rugs and embroidered cushions seem to have been no-cost options on the Maestro at the time. Most probable colours: Beige; Dark Blue; Brown.

The Citroen 2CV

Fabled for its half-minute slog to 60 mph (which was nearly top whack). Seriously sluggard. Greenpeace stickers ritually adorn rear window. Lentil-eating driver. Most probable colours: Yellow; Burgundy and Cream

The VW Camper

House on wheels with dynamics to match. Weird-beard at the wheel makes it effectively a 2CV with a sink. Most probable colour: Orange

Any Lada or Skoda

Skodas and Ladas suffer heavily from automotive snobbery. Drivers of Y-reg Metros and D-reg-last-time-around Beetles will attempt to overtake even the most feisty N-reg Skoda. Drivers duffel-coated. Most probable colour: White

The Reliant Robin

Indistinguishable from spaz-chariots when painted light blue. Driver either fuckwit ex-motorcyclist who can't manage to get a full licence or tight old bastard who wants his 'motoring' as cheap as humanly possible.

Caravans

Invented by a sadist. Design not only to be shit-slow on the road, but a sod to overtake with it. Long and wide. Irremovable net curtain for rear window eliminates tow car visibility, preventing those caravanners who aren't twats (both of them) from pulling over to let following traffic through.

Buses

Normally overtaken when signalling to pull-out. See BUS.

Tractors, JCBs, lorries and other infuriatingly slow vehicles

Obviously.

P

'Pillar'

PARKING

Boy Racers don't pride themselves on their parking skills. So what if you can guide a car into a gap with your wings still intact? It might be useful in Sainsbury's car park but it's not going to get Frank Williams knocking on your door.

Boy Racers prefer to do a 'Bodie and Doyle' – ditch the car and peg it (see PROFESSIONALS, THE).

PEDALS

You should have three of them, drilled aluminium if possible. Two pedals mean an automatic or a pedalo – both of which are wank.

Two pedals bad. Three pedals good.

PEDESTRIAN

Two types of pedestrian are particularly despised by Boy Racers:

Cocky shites who cross the road languidly with a 'you-wouldn't-dare-run-me-over' nonchalance;

Gits who press the button at traffic lights with no intention of crossing.

Both make a convincing argument for bullbars.

PERFORMANCE DRIVING

The art of fast motoring. Boy Racers practice a crude variant, embellished with testosterone charged displays of laddishness. Pure performance driving, however, is much more technical and includes a number of specialist techniques:

HEELING AND TOEING. The heel of the right foot is used to blip the accelerator whilst the sole depresses the brake pedal – which means you end up sitting like Stephen Hawking. Used when changing down the box (either for a power downchange or when double declutching).

POWER DOWNCHANGE. Revving the engine with the clutch in, just before you move into a lower gear. Philistines reckon you've fluffed the change, but smoother cog-swapping results.

DOUBLE DECLUTCHING. Ludicrously complicated method of shifting down a ratio. Essential with cars that don't have a synchromesh gearbox. Like a power downchange except that you select neutral, engage the clutch, rev the engine, disengage the clutch, then move into the lower gear. OK?

LEFT FOOT BRAKING. Used by rally drivers to get the tail out. Stick to the handbrake unless you can speak Scando.

PETROL

see FUEL

PILLAR

1) Strut supporting the roof of a car
2) Where a cockney rests his head at night
3) That fit Spanish bird off the extinct soap *Eldorado*

PLASTIC, BROWN

Ironically, the choice of upholstery for the Austin Leyland Maxi – the least likely car to weaken your bowels with its performance.

POLICE CAR, FOLLOWING

Nothing improves your driving like a police car following you (unless you're a joyrider).

POWER STEERING

Soft option specified by women.

PROBLEM PAGE

The advice clinic is a regular feature of the car magazine. An example of some correspondence with Dr Darren is given below:

Dr
Darren

Dear Dr Darren,
I have a very glamorous job driving over-powered fanny-magnets for a well-known Grand Prix team. Although I do alright for myself – and have a bev with Murray Walker after each race – people reckon that I'm dead boring and only in the game because of my World Champion Dad. Please help. Even little old ladies in Metros are trying to burn me off at the lights.
Damon, Somewhere Nice

Dr Darren replies:
Have you considered fitting a set of Spaxo shocks? Not only do they lower your car by a few inches, but they can do wonders for your roadholding, too. A K&N filter might liberate a few more horsepower – but it really needs to be used in conjunction with a competition exhaust for full effect.

P.S. Try growing a moustache.

Dear Dr Darren,
My fully-lowered and bodykitted XR3i has a gas-flowed turbo unit fitted. The nitrous injection pushes the power up to 500bhp, and the brakes have been uprated to four-pot AP units all-round. A strut-brace and neon number plate surround complete the package. Do you recommend any more modifications?
Paul, Somewhere Sad

Dr Darren replies:
Have you considered fitting another set of Spaxo shocks? Not only will they lower your car even further, but they'll do a little bit more for your roadholding, too. An extra K&N filter might liberate a few more horsepower – but it really needs to be used in conjunction with an additional competition exhaust for full effect.

P.S. Where did you get that number plate surround?

Dear Dr Darren,
Thanks for the plug. The cheque's in the post.
See you at the Round Table on Thursday.
Jim, Spaxo Shock Absorbers Ltd.

Dr Darren replies:
Oh f***.

PRODUCER

If a Boy Racer tells you that he was tugged last night and then got a producer, he either:

Got pulled over by the police, and has to declare some motoring documentation to the local copshop;
or
He's become involved in the pornographic film industry.

PROFESSIONALS, THE

Crime-fighters who used to abandon their Capri rather than go to the bother of parking it properly. Quite unlucky, seeing as how they were always driving in the wrong direction when a call came through to do a handbrake turn every time (being forced).

'Q-Car'

Q-CAR

Most Boy Racers spend a lifetime trying to make their cars look faster than they really are. Grippy Yokohama rubber that stalls the 1.3 mill on take off, bodykits so bewinged that they were obviously a product of Claire Raynor Design and carbon-fibre sticky-back plastic – all conspire to fool onlookers as to the true nature of the Escort beneath.

Q-cars, however, are the complete opposite. They are made to look slower.

This apparent modesty is simply a cover for the real reason of the driver wanting to amuse himself by pissing on machinery that he's caught out.

Simply removing badges that give away a powerful engine could warrant your car a Q-car, but the shoehorning of Rover V8s into Reliant Robins and Citroen 2CVs has been known.

QUEUE

Line of traffic which moves slower than a continental plate. Boy Racers will endeavour to join a queue as late as possible, charging past near-stationary traffic to edge in just before the lane disappears.

R

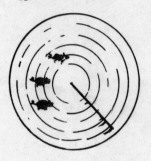

'Radar'

RADAR DETECTOR

Compact scanning device which warns of
nearby police radar activity – either by beeping
or by flashing one of its many red LEDs.
Owning a radar detector is not illegal, but
using one is against the law. Go for a model
which turns itself off when it hears the words
'Is this your car, Sir?'.

RECOVERY SERVICE

Some motoring organisations set up shop at
motorway service stations, but the poor old
bastard on duty always gets ignored. In fact, he
looks such a sorry sight with his patio table
and chairs that he's more likely to attract spare
change than customers.

RED MIST

Adrenalin-induced feeling of invulnerability.
Boy Racers drive under the influence.

ROAD RAGE

There's nothing worse than inconsiderate,
irresponsible, dangerous driving. Which is why
road rage was invented. If everyone took the
trouble to pull over and lamp someone with

suspect motoring habits, the world would be a safer place. For the under 50s, at least.

ROLL

Crash named after a foodstuff. Also see T-BONE.

RIP-SNORTING

See WORDS THAT MOTORING
   JOURNALISTS MAKE UP

RUBBERNECKERS

Like Boy Racers, but they watch the accident from outside the wreckage.

RUST

Unprotected steel rusts in the presence of air and water. You don't need to have spent the last few years in a chemistry lab watching nails in test-tubes to work that one out. But if you did, you may have noticed that it was the nail made in 1970s Italy that rusted first.

S

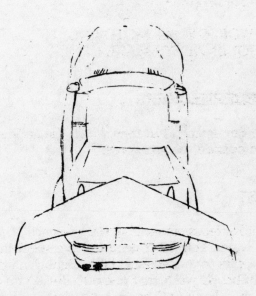

'Spoiler'

SAFETY

Safety sells, so most new cars sport a full range of life-saving devices as standard. Safety systems are either active or passive (which probably means that some either work and others don't).

SECURITY

Security: Bulky key fobs mark the most effective systems.

Car security ranges from Fort Knox to Fort Ileftitlocked.
Here are a few security measures you should know about:

THE LOCKING PETROL CAP.
Essential if you want to stop pilferers from siphoning your petrol away via a hosepipe. Less essential if you don't want a hole drilled in the bottom of the tank instead.

LOCKING WHEEL NUTS.
Prevent the wheels being removed . . . most
likely by the owner in the event of a puncture.

STEERING WHEEL CLAMPS.
These reinforce the internal steering lock,
rendering it impossible for the steering wheel
to be turned. Krooklok brand very popular, but
not with those who think that the English
language is in decline.

GEAR LOCKS.
Disable the car by substantially reducing the
movement of the gear stick. Often thwarted by
removing the gear knob or joyriding in reverse.

WHEEL CLAMPS.
Popularised by the Metropolitan Police, the
wheel clamp is one of the most effective theft
deterrents around. A set of four 'Denver Boots'
is also the ultimate defence against traffic
wardens – clampers can't get you if all the
wheels have been done already.

PET TARANTULA.
An empty tin and a few 'Tarantalarm Arachnid
Patrol' stickers are all that's needed to scare
away thieves. The spider is optional but the
break-in won't be.

HIGH VOLTAGE BODYWORK.
The most illegal anti-theft device as well as the
most effective. Charging the exterior
metalwork up to 10 000 volts protects against
sticky finger-marks as well.

SKID

The result of getting a car out of shape – as frightened passengers will testify.

SLEEPING POLICEMEN

Speed humps are designed to calm traffic by ripping off your front air dam and shagging your suspension if taken at more than 5mph. This doesn't stop Boy Racers from maxing the car between them, though.

SPARKPLUG

As anyone with a Haynes manual knows, close examination of your sparkplugs can be revealing. Consult the following table:

APPEARANCE OF CONTACTS	REASON/ACTION
Black and oily	Engine on its way out. Flog car to your mate before it's too far gone.
Greyish-brown	OK
Dry, black and sooty	Fuel mixture too rich. Add a bit of water. (Only joking.)
Glazed and white	Plug overheating – whatever that means. Get a photographer from Autotrader round just in case.
Fused into a sort of cylindrical thingy	You're looking at the wrong end, Dicksplash. Turn it the other way up.

SPEED

Your speed is influenced by a number of external factors:

Factor	Effect on speed
Car wanting to overtake (following)	+ 10 mph
Police car (following)	– 20 mph
Recent accident visible from road	– 30 mph
Z-bend	nil
Passenger	+ 10 mph
Enthusiastic passenger	+ 20 mph
Pedestrian crossing	nil
Large puddle near bus queue	+ 5 mph
Elderly People Crossing sign	nil

SPOILER

Aerodynamic aid, the size of which is frequently interpreted as being directly proportional to the size of the driver's manhood. By the driver.

STEERING

Boy Racers should ensure that a sports steering wheel is fitted, and that it is handled in the correct manner:

With the elbow resting on some part of the door's structure, the wheel should be lightly gripped with the right hand. The left hand should be affixed to the gear knob or the stereo controls.

This means that a true Boy Racer will never commit the crime of crossing his arms when steering – he should never have had both hands on the wheel in the first place.

Of course, no-handed steering looks even more impressive. Especially when negotiating a roundabout.

Also see POWER STEERING

STOPPING DISTANCE

A few feet longer than the amount of road you've got left. Bugger.

T

'Traffic Jam'

T-BONE

Crash named after a foodstuff. Also see ROLL.

TAILGATING

Following the car in front inches from its rear bumper. See BUNCHING.

TAXI

Like a prostitute – you pay twenty quid for a ride that only lasts a few minutes.

That said, at least you're not the one getting screwed when you have a pro.

TDS

Name given to the mind-numbing Vauxhall Vectra Diesel. You cocked up, boys!

TEST DRIVING

- The work of a bloke employed by a car manufacturer to thrash their latest model into the tarmac (to make sure that it's boring enough to drive for general consumption).

- The opportunity to act like the bloke overleaf in somebody else's car before:

   a) buying an unabused example;
   or
   b) fobbing off the salesman because you were only after the free gift.

TOLLS

Modern day highwaymen bastards. Any essential bridge or tunnel will probably suffer from this form of taxation.

Where there's an extra-heavy toll on your side of the road only, beat the system by reversing along the free carriageway going the other way.

TOTAL

Total damage – a write-off.

TRAFFIC JAM

See QUEUE

TRAFFIC LIGHTS

Boy Racers have their own interpretation of light signals:

SIGNAL	MEANING
RED ALONE	Proceed if travelling too quickly to stop (preferably if the lights have just changed). Otherwise, stop and inch forward impatiently, engine revving. Frighten pedestrians and show off to driver in left lane by increasing revs to 6000rpm in anticipation of impending clutch-dumping start.
RED AND AMBER	Go! Burn off from the lights amidst excessive wheelspin. Gain an advantage over the driver on your left who was 'slow to start'. Swear at traffic which has not yet cleared junction.
GREEN	You should be through the junction by this stage. Green is the signal for the Grandad to release the handbrake and roll back a foot.
AMBER ALONE	As ardent amber gamblers, Boy Racers will try and make the lights. Accelerate hard.

TRIBE

Boy Racing gang that meets in car parks for a CRUISE (qv) whenever they're not too busy mooning. Membership requirements vary, but being able to light your own guffs and not driving a 2CV seem to be pretty universal.

TUNER

Bloke with a pony-tail and beer gut who presides over a 'motorsport centre' – a Santa's Grotto for Boy Racers dedicated to stick-on bodyparts and engine mods. Proof that God owns a Pit Bull, sorry – Staffordshire, terrier and can knock out a respray in a lunchtime.

TURBO

Spinny turbine thing that winds up with the exhaust, forcing air down the engine's neck. Punches you in the back when it comes on boost, which can't be a bad thing (unless you're driving a 2wd Cossie around a wet roundabout at the time).

The time taken for the turbo to spool up is called 'lag' and tends to become noticeable when you've pulled out to overtake something. It is the reason why you think you're going to die.

TWO SECOND RULE, ONLY A FOOL BREAKS THE

Winning entry in a What Cardigan? competition to find an easily-remembered road safety slogan. The runner up (*'Only a c**t tailgates the car in front'*) is less well known.

TYRES

Go for the wide, low-profile ones that look like they've been spread onto the rims with a knife. Why they should be replaced when the tread disappears is a mystery. Everyone knows that slicks have more grip.

U

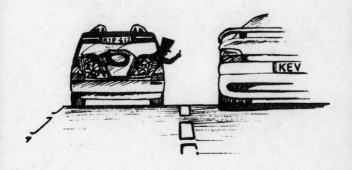

'Undertaking'

U-TURN

A manoeuvre of reasonable laddishness. (If executed blind, using the handbrake.)

UNDERTAKING

Overtaking on the inside. Dangerous enough to keep the namesake profession busy.

UNDERTRAY

Flattish bit on the bottom of a car that collects carrier bags if you attempt to drive over them.

V

'Vent'

VSE

Volvo Spongiform Encephalopathy. Identified
after years of painstaking research into the
driving behaviour of Volvo owners. The first
symptoms of this horrific disease manifest
themselves in forgetfulness (leaving the
foglights on after a misty patch, perhaps).
Dizzy spells and a loss of coordination occur in
more advanced cases, although the complete
cessation of bodily functions is mercifully rare
(every bank holiday, or so).

VAN

Goods vehicle normally driven with an
enthusiasm reserved for someone else's
property (also see HIRE CARS). Quicker when
there are three lads in the front, for some
reason.

VASCAR

In-car video camera used in police cars. Worth
trying to get a copy of the tape if you've been
done after doing something decent. Don't worry
if you can't – if it's that good it'll be on Police
Camera Action.

VELOUR

Popular cloth trim. Changes colour when brushed the wrong way, therefore making it possible to write offensive words on the seats. (Permanent messages require the use of an electric shaver.)

VENT

Debris trapped in the ventilation system can be a good indication as to the efficiency of the filter. Leaves and dead wasps are acceptable, but hedgehogs are worrying.

VITESSE

Poofy French word for 'speed'.

W

'Wheel . . .'

WEATHER

Most motorists alter their driving style to suit the weather. Boy Racers are no exception:

WEATHER CONDITIONS	DRIVING STYLE
Fair	Right foot welded to the floor.
Overcast	Right foot welded to the floor. Sidelights on.
Sunny	Right foot welded to the floor. Sunvisor down.
Rainy	Right foot welded to the floor. Wipers on.
Fog and mist	Right foot welded to the floor. Foglights on.

WHEELS, ALLOY

Attractive because of their light weight (you won't get a hernia nicking them). The less spokes the better, but don't paint them gold (unless you're gay).

WHEEL CLAMP

see SECURITY

WINDSCREEN

Pane of glass you look out of to see where you're going. Owners of two-wheel drive Cosworths find that theirs wind down.

'X-Files'

X-FILES

Mysterious top secret government files. Topics covered range from why spare wheels are always covered in shit, through to the alleged sighting of a 'standard' Reliant Robin doing 108mph on the motorway.

One Allegro driver who was abducted by aliens told of strange experiments and bizarre sex. The aliens were astounded.

XR3i

Legendary Ford hot hatch. Fairly quick, begging to be modified and quite good value (even better value when stolen). Now detuned and badged as an 'Si', which is akin to your best mate coming out.

X's NEW BOYFRIEND

Why you mounted the pavement outside the cinema last Friday.

Y

'Yin-Yang Ethno-Beads'

YELLOW

Top colour. Not for shy and retiring types, but
there's nothing wrong with that. In fact, you've
got to be a bit of a cocky gobshite with more
front than what's good for you, really. Suits
Corrados, Intergrowlers and AA vans.

YIN-YANG ETHNO-BEADS

Hippy bollocks slagged off first time around
under ACCESSORIES.

Z

'ZZZZZZ'

ZEBRA CROSSING

Pedestrian right of way. If you can be bothered
to stop.
Also see ACCELERATOR.

ZZZZZZ
See CAR BORE

DISCLAIMER

Kevin Court wishes for it to be known that he accepts no responsibility for anybody else's nutty driving. He has a hard enough time keeping himself out of trouble without you landing him in the shit.

PUBLISHER'S NOTE

The Boy Racer's Handbook is observational only, and does not prescribe the reckless driving that Kilroy reckons it advocates. Neither does it condone dangerous driving or violations of Traffic Law. It is *not* a technical driving manual. If you want to know how to pass your test, buy *Roadcraft* (and a tank top while you're at it).